ARE YOU TAKING A TRIP?

Use this journal to record the memories you make during vacations.

With different pages on vacation planning, journal writing, exploration reports, scrapbooking and sketching, you can always come back to your vacation memories even after the adventure is over!

VACATION PLANNING

Places I want to see	Things I want to do	Food I want to eat

VACATION PLANNING

I've always wanted to...

in the exciting place called...

I will bring these stuff with me:

- [ ]
- [ ]
- [ ]
- [ ]
- [ ]

People and pets who will be with me:

- [ ]
- [ ]
- [ ]
- [ ]
- [ ]

We will travel by:

When do you want to go on this trip?

Draw a picture of what you want to do in your vacation:

LAKE

TRAILS

RESORT

VACATION PLANNING

I've always wanted to...

in the exciting place called...

I will bring these stuff with me:

- [ ] _____
- [ ] _____
- [ ] _____
- [ ] _____
- [ ] _____

People and pets who will be with me:

- [ ] _____
- [ ] _____
- [ ] _____
- [ ] _____
- [ ] _____

We will travel by:

When do you want to go on this trip?

Draw a picture of what you want to do in your vacation:

VACATION PLANNING

I've always wanted to...

in the exciting place called...

I will bring these stuff with me:

- [ ] _____
- [ ] _____
- [ ] _____
- [ ] _____
- [ ] _____

People and pets who will be with me:

- [ ] _____
- [ ] _____
- [ ] _____
- [ ] _____
- [ ] _____

We will travel by:

When do you want to go on this trip?

Draw a picture of what you want to do in your vacation:

LAKE

TRAILS

RESORT

VACATION PLANNING

I've always wanted to...

in the exciting place called...

I will bring these stuff with me:

- [ ] _____
- [ ] _____
- [ ] _____
- [ ] _____
- [ ] _____

People and pets who will be with me:

- [ ] _____
- [ ] _____
- [ ] _____
- [ ] _____
- [ ] _____

We will travel by:

When do you want to go on this trip?

Draw a picture of what you want to do in your vacation:

VACATION PLANNING

I've always wanted to...

in the exciting place called...

I will bring these stuff with me:

- [ ] _____
- [ ] _____
- [ ] _____
- [ ] _____
- [ ] _____

People and pets who will be with me:

- [ ] _____
- [ ] _____
- [ ] _____
- [ ] _____
- [ ] _____

We will travel by:

When do you want to go on this trip?

Draw a picture of what you want to do in your vacation:

LAKE

TRAILS

RESORT

VACATION PLANNING

I've always wanted to...

in the exciting place called...

I will bring these stuff with me:

- ☐ _____
- ☐ _____
- ☐ _____
- ☐ _____
- ☐ _____

People and pets who will be with me:

- ☐ _____
- ☐ _____
- ☐ _____
- ☐ _____
- ☐ _____

We will travel by:

When do you want to go on this trip?

Draw a picture of what you want to do in your vacation:

VACATION PLANNING

I've always wanted to...

in the exciting place called...

I will bring these stuff with me:

- [ ]
- [ ]
- [ ]
- [ ]
- [ ]

People and pets who will be with me:

- [ ]
- [ ]
- [ ]
- [ ]
- [ ]

We will travel by:

When do you want to go on this trip?

Draw a picture of what you want to do in your vacation:

LAKE →

← TRAILS

RESORT →

VACATION PLANNING

I've always wanted to...

in the exciting place called...

I will bring these stuff with me:

- ☐
- ☐
- ☐
- ☐
- ☐

People and pets who will be with me:

- ☐
- ☐
- ☐
- ☐
- ☐

We will travel by:

When do you want to go on this trip?

Draw a picture of what you want to do in your vacation:

VACATION PLANNING

I've always wanted to...

in the exciting place called...

I will bring these stuff with me:

- [ ] _____
- [ ] _____
- [ ] _____
- [ ] _____
- [ ] _____

People and pets who will be with me:

- [ ] _____
- [ ] _____
- [ ] _____
- [ ] _____
- [ ] _____

We will travel by:

When do you want to go on this trip?

Draw a picture of what you want to do in your vacation:

LAKE

TRAILS

RESORT

VACATION PLANNING

I've always wanted to...

in the exciting place called...

I will bring these stuff with me:

- [ ] _____
- [ ] _____
- [ ] _____
- [ ] _____
- [ ] _____

People and pets who will be with me:

- [ ] _____
- [ ] _____
- [ ] _____
- [ ] _____
- [ ] _____

We will travel by:

When do you want to go on this trip?

Draw a picture of what you want to do in your vacation:

VACATION PLANNING

I've always wanted to...

in the exciting place called...

I will bring these stuff with me:

- ☐ _____
- ☐ _____
- ☐ _____
- ☐ _____
- ☐ _____

People and pets who will be with me:

- ☐ _____
- ☐ _____
- ☐ _____
- ☐ _____
- ☐ _____

We will travel by:

When do you want to go on this trip?

Draw a picture of what you want to do in your vacation:

LAKE

TRAILS

RESORT

VACATION PLANNING

I've always wanted to...

in the exciting place called...

I will bring these stuff with me:

- [ ] _____
- [ ] _____
- [ ] _____
- [ ] _____
- [ ] _____

People and pets who will be with me:

- [ ] _____
- [ ] _____
- [ ] _____
- [ ] _____
- [ ] _____

We will travel by:

When do you want to go on this trip?

Draw a picture of what you want to do in your vacation:

VACATION PLANNING

I've always wanted to...

in the exciting place called...

I will bring these stuff with me:

- [ ]
- [ ]
- [ ]
- [ ]
- [ ]

People and pets who will be with me:

- [ ]
- [ ]
- [ ]
- [ ]
- [ ]

We will travel by:

When do you want to go on this trip?

Draw a picture of what you want to do in your vacation:

LAKE

TRAILS

RESORT

VACATION PLANNING

I've always wanted to...

in the exciting place called...

I will bring these stuff with me:

- ☐ _____
- ☐ _____
- ☐ _____
- ☐ _____
- ☐ _____

People and pets who will be with me:

- ☐ _____
- ☐ _____
- ☐ _____
- ☐ _____
- ☐ _____

We will travel by:

When do you want to go on this trip?

Draw a picture of what you want to do in your vacation:

VACATION PLANNING

I've always wanted to...

in the exciting place called...

I will bring these stuff with me:

- [ ]
- [ ]
- [ ]
- [ ]
- [ ]

People and pets who will be with me:

- [ ]
- [ ]
- [ ]
- [ ]
- [ ]

We will travel by:

When do you want to go on this trip?

Draw a picture of what you want to do in your vacation:

LAKE

TRAILS

RESORT

VACATION PLANNING

I've always wanted to...

in the exciting place called...

I will bring these stuff with me:

- ☐ _____
- ☐ _____
- ☐ _____
- ☐ _____
- ☐ _____

People and pets who will be with me:

- ☐ _____
- ☐ _____
- ☐ _____
- ☐ _____
- ☐ _____

We will travel by:

When do you want to go on this trip?

Draw a picture of what you want to do in your vacation:

VACATION PLANNING

I've always wanted to...

in the exciting place called...

I will bring these stuff with me:

- [ ] _____
- [ ] _____
- [ ] _____
- [ ] _____
- [ ] _____

People and pets who will be with me:

- [ ] _____
- [ ] _____
- [ ] _____
- [ ] _____
- [ ] _____

We will travel by:

When do you want to go on this trip?

Draw a picture of what you want to do in your vacation:

LAKE

TRAILS

RESORT

VACATION PLANNING

I've always wanted to...

in the exciting place called...

I will bring these stuff with me:

- ☐ _____
- ☐ _____
- ☐ _____
- ☐ _____
- ☐ _____

People and pets who will be with me:

- ☐ _____
- ☐ _____
- ☐ _____
- ☐ _____
- ☐ _____

We will travel by:

When do you want to go on this trip?

Draw a picture of what you want to do in your vacation:

VACATION PLANNING

I've always wanted to...

in the exciting place called...

I will bring these stuff with me:

- [ ]
- [ ]
- [ ]
- [ ]
- [ ]

People and pets who will be with me:

- [ ]
- [ ]
- [ ]
- [ ]
- [ ]

We will travel by:

When do you want to go on this trip?

Draw a picture of what you want to do in your vacation:

LAKE

TRAILS

RESORT

VACATION PLANNING

I've always wanted to...

in the exciting place called...

I will bring these stuff with me:

- ☐ _____
- ☐ _____
- ☐ _____
- ☐ _____
- ☐ _____

People and pets who will be with me:

- ☐ _____
- ☐ _____
- ☐ _____
- ☐ _____
- ☐ _____

We will travel by:

When do you want to go on this trip?

Draw a picture of what you want to do in your vacation:

VACATION PLANNING

I've always wanted to...

in the exciting place called...

I will bring these stuff with me:

- ☐ _____
- ☐ _____
- ☐ _____
- ☐ _____
- ☐ _____

People and pets who will be with me:

- ☐ _____
- ☐ _____
- ☐ _____
- ☐ _____
- ☐ _____

We will travel by:

When do you want to go on this trip?

Draw a picture of what you want to do in your vacation:

LAKE —

TRAILS

RESORT

VACATION PLANNING

I've always wanted to...

in the exciting place called...

I will bring these stuff with me:

- [ ]
- [ ]
- [ ]
- [ ]
- [ ]

People and pets who will be with me:

- [ ]
- [ ]
- [ ]
- [ ]
- [ ]

We will travel by:

When do you want to go on this trip?

Draw a picture of what you want to do in your vacation:

VACATION PLANNING

I've always wanted to...

in the exciting place called...

I will bring these stuff with me:

- [ ]
- [ ]
- [ ]
- [ ]
- [ ]

People and pets who will be with me:

- [ ]
- [ ]
- [ ]
- [ ]
- [ ]

We will travel by:

When do you want to go on this trip?

Draw a picture of what you want to do in your vacation:

VACATION PLANNING

I've always wanted to...

in the exciting place called...

I will bring these stuff with me:

People and pets who will be with me:

We will travel by:

When do you want to go on this trip?

Draw a picture of what you want to do in your vacation:

VACATION PLANNING

I've always wanted to...

in the exciting place called...

I will bring these stuff with me:

- ☐ _____
- ☐ _____
- ☐ _____
- ☐ _____
- ☐ _____

People and pets who will be with me:

- ☐ _____
- ☐ _____
- ☐ _____
- ☐ _____
- ☐ _____

We will travel by:

When do you want to go on this trip?

Draw a picture of what you want to do in your vacation:

VACATION PLANNING

I've always wanted to...

in the exciting place called...

I will bring these stuff with me:

- [ ]
- [ ]
- [ ]
- [ ]
- [ ]

People and pets who will be with me:

- [ ]
- [ ]
- [ ]
- [ ]
- [ ]

We will travel by:

When do you want to go on this trip?

Draw a picture of what you want to do in your vacation:

VACATION PLANNING

I've always wanted to...

in the exciting place called...

I will bring these stuff with me:

- [ ] _____
- [ ] _____
- [ ] _____
- [ ] _____
- [ ] _____

People and pets who will be with me:

- [ ] _____
- [ ] _____
- [ ] _____
- [ ] _____
- [ ] _____

We will travel by:

When do you want to go on this trip?

Draw a picture of what you want to do in your vacation:

LAKE →

← TRAILS

RESORT →

VACATION PLANNING

I've always wanted to...

in the exciting place called...

I will bring these stuff with me:

- [ ]
- [ ]
- [ ]
- [ ]
- [ ]

People and pets who will be with me:

- [ ]
- [ ]
- [ ]
- [ ]
- [ ]

We will travel by:

When do you want to go on this trip?

Draw a picture of what you want to do in your vacation:

VACATION PLANNING

I've always wanted to...

in the exciting place called...

I will bring these stuff with me:

- ☐ _____
- ☐ _____
- ☐ _____
- ☐ _____
- ☐ _____

People and pets who will be with me:

- ☐ _____
- ☐ _____
- ☐ _____
- ☐ _____
- ☐ _____

We will travel by:

When do you want to go on this trip?

Draw a picture of what you want to do in your vacation:

LAKE →

← TRAILS

RESORT →

VACATION PLANNING

I've always wanted to...

in the exciting place called...

I will bring these stuff with me:

- [ ] _____
- [ ] _____
- [ ] _____
- [ ] _____
- [ ] _____

People and pets who will be with me:

- [ ] _____
- [ ] _____
- [ ] _____
- [ ] _____
- [ ] _____

We will travel by:

When do you want to go on this trip?

Draw a picture of what you want to do in your vacation:

VACATION PLANNING

I've always wanted to...

in the exciting place called...

I will bring these stuff with me:

- ☐ _____
- ☐ _____
- ☐ _____
- ☐ _____
- ☐ _____

People and pets who will be with me:

- ☐ _____
- ☐ _____
- ☐ _____
- ☐ _____
- ☐ _____

We will travel by:

When do you want to go on this trip?

Draw a picture of what you want to do in your vacation:

LAKE

TRAILS

RESORT

JOURNAL WRITING

MY VACATION IN...

OVERALL RATING:

Tell us a story abour your vacation. WHEN did you go on your trip? WHERE did you visit? WHO were you with? WHAT did you do?

  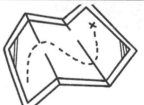

MY EXPLORATION REPORT:

During vacation, what was the weather like?

_____

_____

Listen closely. What 3 nature sounds can you hear?

1 _____

2 _____

3 _____

Look around. What 3 animals or insects do you see?

1 _____

2 _____

3 _____

Did you see a body of water? What was it like?

_____

_____

Did you see buildings or houses? What were they like?

_____

_____

_____

What is unique about this vacation?

Paste, draw, doodle or write evidence of your exploration here:

What were the top 5 activities you did in the national park?

1 _____

2 _____

3 _____

4 _____

5 _____

JOURNAL WRITING

MY VACATION IN...

OVERALL RATING:

Tell us a story abour your vacation. WHEN did you go on your trip? WHERE did you visit? WHO were you with? WHAT did you do?

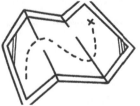

MY EXPLORATION REPORT:

During vacation, what was the weather like?

_____

_____

Listen closely. What 3 nature sounds can you hear?

1 _____

2 _____

3 _____

Look around. What 3 animals or insects do you see?

1 _____

2 _____

3 _____

Did you see a body of water? What was it like?

_____

_____

Did you see buildings or houses? What were they like?

_____

_____

_____

What is unique about this vacation?

What were the top 5 activities you did in the national park?

1 _____

2 _____

3 _____

4 _____

5 _____

Paste, draw, doodle or write evidence of your exploration here:

JOURNAL WRITING

MY VACATION IN...

OVERALL RATING:

Tell us a story abour your vacation. WHEN did you go on your trip? WHERE did you visit? WHO were you with? WHAT did you do?

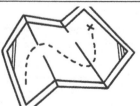

MY EXPLORATION REPORT:

During vacation, what was the weather like?

_____

_____

Listen closely. What 3 nature sounds can you hear?

1 _____

2 _____

3 _____

Look around. What 3 animals or insects do you see?

1 _____

2 _____

3 _____

Did you see a body of water? What was it like?

_____

_____

Did you see buildings or houses? What were they like?

_____

_____

_____

What is unique about this vacation?

What were the top 5 activities you did in the national park?

1 _____

2 _____

3 _____

4 _____

5 _____

Paste, draw, doodle or write evidence of your exploration here:

JOURNAL WRITING

MY VACATION IN...

OVERALL RATING:

Tell us a story abour your vacation. WHEN did you go on your trip? WHERE did you visit? WHO were you with? WHAT did you do?

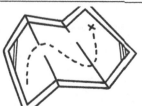

MY EXPLORATION REPORT:

During vacation, what was the weather like?

_____

_____

Listen closely. What 3 nature sounds can you hear?

1 _____

2 _____

3 _____

Look around. What 3 animals or insects do you see?

1 _____

2 _____

3 _____

Did you see a body of water? What was it like?

_____

_____

Did you see buildings or houses? What were they like?

_____

_____

_____

What is unique about this vacation?

Paste, draw, doodle or write evidence of your exploration here:

What were the top 5 activities you did in the national park?

1 _____

2 _____

3 _____

4 _____

5 _____

JOURNAL WRITING

MY VACATION IN...

OVERALL RATING:

Tell us a story abour your vacation. WHEN did you go on your trip? WHERE did you visit? WHO were you with? WHAT did you do?

MY EXPLORATION REPORT:

During vacation, what was the weather like?

_____

_____

Listen closely. What 3 nature sounds can you hear?

1 _____

2 _____

3 _____

Look around. What 3 animals or insects do you see?

1 _____

2 _____

3 _____

Did you see a body of water? What was it like?

_____

_____

Did you see buildings or houses? What were they like?

_____

_____

_____

What is unique about this vacation?

What were the top 5 activities you did in the national park?

1 _____

2 _____

3 _____

4 _____

5 _____

Paste, draw, doodle or write evidence of your exploration here:

JOURNAL WRITING

MY VACATION IN...

OVERALL RATING:

Tell us a story abour your vacation. WHEN did you go on your trip? WHERE did you visit? WHO were you with? WHAT did you do?

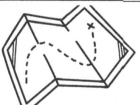

MY EXPLORATION REPORT:

During vacation, what was the weather like?

_____

_____

Listen closely. What 3 nature sounds can you hear?

1 _____

2 _____

3 _____

Look around. What 3 animals or insects do you see?

1 _____

2 _____

3 _____

Did you see a body of water? What was it like?

_____

_____

Did you see buildings or houses? What were they like?

_____

_____

_____

What is unique about this vacation?

What were the top 5 activities you did in the national park?

1 _____

2 _____

3 _____

4 _____

5 _____

Paste, draw, doodle or write evidence of your exploration here:

JOURNAL WRITING

MY VACATION IN...

OVERALL RATING:

Tell us a story abour your vacation. WHEN did you go on your trip? WHERE did you visit? WHO were you with? WHAT did you do?

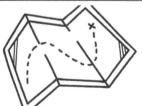

MY EXPLORATION REPORT:

During vacation, what was the weather like?

_____

_____

Listen closely. What 3 nature sounds can you hear?

1 _____

2 _____

3 _____

Look around. What 3 animals or insects do you see?

1 _____

2 _____

3 _____

Did you see a body of water? What was it like?

_____

_____

Did you see buildings or houses? What were they like?

_____

_____

_____

What is unique about this vacation?

What were the top 5 activities you did in the national park?

1 _____

2 _____

3 _____

4 _____

5 _____

Paste, draw, doodle or write evidence of your exploration here:

JOURNAL WRITING

MY VACATION IN...

OVERALL RATING:

Tell us a story abour your vacation. WHEN did you go on your trip? WHERE did you visit? WHO were you with? WHAT did you do?

MY EXPLORATION REPORT:

During vacation, what was the weather like?

_____

_____

Listen closely. What 3 nature sounds can you hear?

1 _____

2 _____

3 _____

Look around. What 3 animals or insects do you see?

1 _____

2 _____

3 _____

Did you see a body of water? What was it like?

_____

_____

Did you see buildings or houses? What were they like?

_____

_____

_____

What is unique about this vacation?

What were the top 5 activities you did in the national park?

1 _____

2 _____

3 _____

4 _____

5 _____

Paste, draw, doodle or write evidence of your exploration here:

JOURNAL WRITING

MY VACATION IN...

OVERALL RATING:

Tell us a story abour your vacation. WHEN did you go on your trip? WHERE did you visit? WHO were you with? WHAT did you do?

MY EXPLORATION REPORT:

During vacation, what was the weather like?

_____

_____

Listen closely. What 3 nature sounds can you hear?

1 _____

2 _____

3 _____

Look around. What 3 animals or insects do you see?

1 _____

2 _____

3 _____

Did you see a body of water? What was it like?

_____

_____

Did you see buildings or houses? What were they like?

_____

_____

_____

What is unique about this vacation?

What were the top 5 activities you did in the national park?

1 _____

2 _____

3 _____

4 _____

5 _____

Paste, draw, doodle or write evidence of your exploration here:

JOURNAL WRITING

MY VACATION IN...

OVERALL RATING:

Tell us a story abour your vacation. WHEN did you go on your trip? WHERE did you visit? WHO were you with? WHAT did you do?

MY EXPLORATION REPORT:

During vacation, what was the weather like?

_____

_____

Listen closely. What 3 nature sounds can you hear?

1 _____

2 _____

3 _____

Look around. What 3 animals or insects do you see?

1 _____

2 _____

3 _____

Did you see a body of water? What was it like?

_____

_____

Did you see buildings or houses? What were they like?

_____

_____

_____

What is unique about this vacation?

What were the top 5 activities you did in the national park?

1 _____

2 _____

3 _____

4 _____

5 _____

Paste, draw, doodle or write evidence of your exploration here:

JOURNAL WRITING

MY VACATION IN...

OVERALL RATING:

Tell us a story abour your vacation. WHEN did you go on your trip? WHERE did you visit? WHO were you with? WHAT did you do?

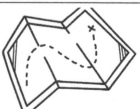

MY EXPLORATION REPORT:

During vacation, what was the weather like?

_____

_____

Listen closely. What 3 nature sounds can you hear?

1 _____

2 _____

3 _____

Look around. What 3 animals or insects do you see?

1 _____

2 _____

3 _____

Did you see a body of water? What was it like?

_____

_____

Did you see buildings or houses? What were they like?

_____

_____

_____

What is unique about this vacation?

What were the top 5 activities you did in the national park?

1 _____

2 _____

3 _____

4 _____

5 _____

Paste, draw, doodle or write evidence of your exploration here:

JOURNAL WRITING

MY VACATION IN...

OVERALL RATING:

Tell us a story abour your vacation. WHEN did you go on your trip? WHERE did you visit? WHO were you with? WHAT did you do?

MY EXPLORATION REPORT:

During vacation, what was the weather like?

_____

_____

Listen closely. What 3 nature sounds can you hear?

1 _____

2 _____

3 _____

Look around. What 3 animals or insects do you see?

1 _____

2 _____

3 _____

Did you see a body of water? What was it like?

_____

_____

Did you see buildings or houses? What were they like?

_____

_____

_____

What is unique about this vacation?

What were the top 5 activities you did in the national park?

1 _____

2 _____

3 _____

4 _____

5 _____

Paste, draw, doodle or write evidence of your exploration here:

JOURNAL WRITING

MY VACATION IN...

OVERALL RATING:

Tell us a story abour your vacation. WHEN did you go on your trip? WHERE did you visit? WHO were you with? WHAT did you do?

MY EXPLORATION REPORT:

During vacation, what was the weather like?

_____

_____

Listen closely. What 3 nature sounds can you hear?

1 _____

2 _____

3 _____

Look around. What 3 animals or insects do you see?

1 _____

2 _____

3 _____

Did you see a body of water? What was it like?

_____

_____

Did you see buildings or houses? What were they like?

_____

_____

_____

What is unique about this vacation?

Paste, draw, doodle or write evidence of your exploration here:

What were the top 5 activities you did in the national park?

1 _____

2 _____

3 _____

4 _____

5 _____

JOURNAL WRITING

MY VACATION IN...

OVERALL RATING:

Tell us a story abour your vacation. WHEN did you go on your trip? WHERE did you visit? WHO were you with? WHAT did you do?

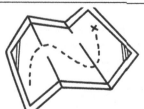

MY EXPLORATION REPORT:

During vacation, what was the weather like?

_____

_____

Listen closely. What 3 nature sounds can you hear?

1 _____

2 _____

3 _____

Look around. What 3 animals or insects do you see?

1 _____

2 _____

3 _____

Did you see a body of water? What was it like?

_____

_____

Did you see buildings or houses? What were they like?

_____

_____

_____

What is unique about this vacation?

Paste, draw, doodle or write evidence of your exploration here:

What were the top 5 activities you did in the national park?

1 _____

2 _____

3 _____

4 _____

5 _____

JOURNAL WRITING

MY VACATION IN...

OVERALL RATING:

Tell us a story abour your vacation. WHEN did you go on your trip? WHERE did you visit? WHO were you with? WHAT did you do?

MY EXPLORATION REPORT:

During vacation, what was the weather like?

_____

_____

Listen closely. What 3 nature sounds can you hear?

1 _____

2 _____

3 _____

Look around. What 3 animals or insects do you see?

1 _____

2 _____

3 _____

Did you see a body of water? What was it like?

_____

_____

Did you see buildings or houses? What were they like?

_____

_____

_____

What is unique about this vacation?

What were the top 5 activities you did in the national park?

1 _____

2 _____

3 _____

4 _____

5 _____

Paste, draw, doodle or write evidence of your exploration here:

JOURNAL WRITING

MY VACATION IN...

OVERALL RATING:

Tell us a story abour your vacation. WHEN did you go on your trip? WHERE did you visit? WHO were you with? WHAT did you do?

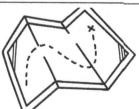

MY EXPLORATION REPORT:

During vacation, what was the weather like?

_____

_____

Listen closely. What 3 nature sounds can you hear?

1 _____

2 _____

3 _____

Look around. What 3 animals or insects do you see?

1 _____

2 _____

3 _____

Did you see a body of water? What was it like?

_____

_____

Did you see buildings or houses? What were they like?

_____

_____

_____

What is unique about this vacation?

What were the top 5 activities you did in the national park?

1 _____

2 _____

3 _____

4 _____

5 _____

Paste, draw, doodle or write evidence of your exploration here:

JOURNAL WRITING

MY VACATION IN...

OVERALL RATING:

Tell us a story abour your vacation. WHEN did you go on your trip? WHERE did you visit? WHO were you with? WHAT did you do?

MY EXPLORATION REPORT:

During vacation, what was the weather like?

_____

_____

Listen closely. What 3 nature sounds can you hear?

1 _____

2 _____

3 _____

Look around. What 3 animals or insects do you see?

1 _____

2 _____

3 _____

Did you see a body of water? What was it like?

_____

_____

Did you see buildings or houses? What were they like?

_____

_____

_____

What is unique about this vacation?

What were the top 5 activities you did in the national park?

1 _____

2 _____

3 _____

4 _____

5 _____

Paste, draw, doodle or write evidence of your exploration here:

JOURNAL WRITING

MY VACATION IN...

OVERALL RATING:

Tell us a story abour your vacation. WHEN did you go on your trip? WHERE did you visit? WHO were you with? WHAT did you do?

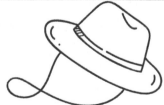

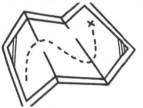

MY EXPLORATION REPORT:

During vacation, what was the weather like?

_____

_____

Listen closely. What 3 nature sounds can you hear?

1 _____

2 _____

3 _____

Look around. What 3 animals or insects do you see?

1 _____

2 _____

3 _____

Did you see a body of water? What was it like?

_____

_____

Did you see buildings or houses? What were they like?

_____

_____

_____

What is unique about this vacation?

Paste, draw, doodle or write evidence of your exploration here:

What were the top 5 activities you did in the national park?

1 _____

2 _____

3 _____

4 _____

5 _____

JOURNAL WRITING

MY VACATION IN...

OVERALL RATING:

Tell us a story abour your vacation. WHEN did you go on your trip? WHERE did you visit? WHO were you with? WHAT did you do?

MY EXPLORATION REPORT:

During vacation, what was the weather like?

_____

_____

Listen closely. What 3 nature sounds can you hear?

1 _____

2 _____

3 _____

Look around. What 3 animals or insects do you see?

1 _____

2 _____

3 _____

Did you see a body of water? What was it like?

_____

_____

Did you see buildings or houses? What were they like?

_____

_____

_____

What is unique about this vacation?

What were the top 5 activities you did in the national park?

1 _____

2 _____

3 _____

4 _____

5 _____

Paste, draw, doodle or write evidence of your exploration here:

JOURNAL WRITING

MY VACATION IN...

OVERALL RATING:

Tell us a story abour your vacation. WHEN did you go on your trip? WHERE did you visit? WHO were you with? WHAT did you do?

_____

_____

_____

_____

_____

_____

_____

_____

_____

_____

_____

_____

_____

_____

_____

_____

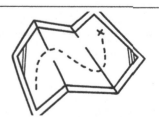

MY EXPLORATION REPORT:

During vacation, what was the weather like?

_____

_____

Listen closely. What 3 nature sounds can you hear?

1 _____

2 _____

3 _____

Look around. What 3 animals or insects do you see?

1 _____

2 _____

3 _____

Did you see a body of water? What was it like?

_____

_____

Did you see buildings or houses? What were they like?

_____

_____

_____

What is unique about this vacation?

What were the top 5 activities you did in the national park?

1 _____

2 _____

3 _____

4 _____

5 _____

Paste, draw, doodle or write evidence of your exploration here:

JOURNAL WRITING

MY VACATION IN...

OVERALL RATING:

Tell us a story abour your vacation. WHEN did you go on your trip? WHERE did you visit? WHO were you with? WHAT did you do?

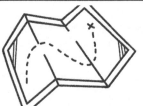

MY EXPLORATION REPORT:

During vacation, what was the weather like?

_____

_____

Listen closely. What 3 nature sounds can you hear?

1 _____

2 _____

3 _____

Look around. What 3 animals or insects do you see?

1 _____

2 _____

3 _____

Did you see a body of water? What was it like?

_____

_____

Did you see buildings or houses? What were they like?

_____

_____

_____

What is unique about this vacation?

What were the top 5 activities you did in the national park?

1 _____

2 _____

3 _____

4 _____

5 _____

Paste, draw, doodle or write evidence of your exploration here:

JOURNAL WRITING

MY VACATION IN...

OVERALL RATING:

Tell us a story abour your vacation. WHEN did you go on your trip? WHERE did you visit? WHO were you with? WHAT did you do?

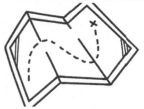

MY EXPLORATION REPORT:

During vacation, what was the weather like?

_____

_____

Listen closely. What 3 nature sounds can you hear?

1 _____

2 _____

3 _____

Look around. What 3 animals or insects do you see?

1 _____

2 _____

3 _____

Did you see a body of water? What was it like?

_____

_____

Did you see buildings or houses? What were they like?

_____

_____

_____

What is unique about this vacation?

What were the top 5 activities you did in the national park?

1 _____

2 _____

3 _____

4 _____

5 _____

Paste, draw, doodle or write evidence of your exploration here:

JOURNAL WRITING

MY VACATION IN...

OVERALL RATING:

Tell us a story abour your vacation. WHEN did you go on your trip? WHERE did you visit? WHO were you with? WHAT did you do?

MY EXPLORATION REPORT:

During vacation, what was the weather like?

_____

_____

Listen closely. What 3 nature sounds can you hear?

1 _____

2 _____

3 _____

Look around. What 3 animals or insects do you see?

1 _____

2 _____

3 _____

Did you see a body of water? What was it like?

_____

_____

Did you see buildings or houses? What were they like?

_____

_____

_____

What is unique about this vacation?

What were the top 5 activities you did in the national park?

1 _____

2 _____

3 _____

4 _____

5 _____

Paste, draw, doodle or write evidence of your exploration here:

JOURNAL WRITING

MY VACATION IN...

OVERALL RATING:

Tell us a story abour your vacation. WHEN did you go on your trip? WHERE did you visit? WHO were you with? WHAT did you do?

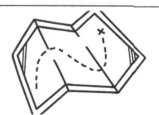

MY EXPLORATION REPORT:

During vacation, what was the weather like?

_____

_____

Listen closely. What 3 nature sounds can you hear?

1 _____

2 _____

3 _____

Look around. What 3 animals or insects do you see?

1 _____

2 _____

3 _____

Did you see a body of water? What was it like?

_____

_____

Did you see buildings or houses? What were they like?

_____

_____

_____

What is unique about this vacation?

What were the top 5 activities you did in the national park?

1 _____

2 _____

3 _____

4 _____

5 _____

Paste, draw, doodle or write evidence of your exploration here:

JOURNAL WRITING

MY VACATION IN...

OVERALL RATING:

Tell us a story abour your vacation. WHEN did you go on your trip? WHERE did you visit? WHO were you with? WHAT did you do?

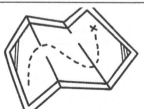

MY EXPLORATION REPORT:

During vacation, what was the weather like?

_____

_____

Listen closely. What 3 nature sounds can you hear?

1 _____

2 _____

3 _____

Look around. What 3 animals or insects do you see?

1 _____

2 _____

3 _____

Did you see a body of water? What was it like?

_____

_____

Did you see buildings or houses? What were they like?

_____

_____

_____

What is unique about this vacation?

What were the top 5 activities you did in the national park?

1 _____

2 _____

3 _____

4 _____

5 _____

Paste, draw, doodle or write evidence of your exploration here:

JOURNAL WRITING

MY VACATION IN...

OVERALL RATING:

Tell us a story abour your vacation. WHEN did you go on your trip? WHERE did you visit? WHO were you with? WHAT did you do?

_____

_____

_____

_____

_____

_____

_____

_____

_____

_____

_____

_____

_____

_____

_____

_____

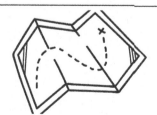

MY EXPLORATION REPORT:

During vacation, what was the weather like?

_____

_____

Listen closely. What 3 nature sounds can you hear?

1 _____

2 _____

3 _____

Look around. What 3 animals or insects do you see?

1 _____

2 _____

3 _____

Did you see a body of water? What was it like?

_____

_____

Did you see buildings or houses? What were they like?

_____

_____

_____

What is unique about this vacation?

Paste, draw, doodle or write evidence of your exploration here:

What were the top 5 activities you did in the national park?

1 _____

2 _____

3 _____

4 _____

5 _____

JOURNAL WRITING

MY VACATION IN...

OVERALL RATING:

Tell us a story abour your vacation. WHEN did you go on your trip? WHERE did you visit? WHO were you with? WHAT did you do?

MY EXPLORATION REPORT:

During vacation, what was the weather like?

_____

_____

Listen closely. What 3 nature sounds can you hear?

1 _____

2 _____

3 _____

Look around. What 3 animals or insects do you see?

1 _____

2 _____

3 _____

Did you see a body of water? What was it like?

_____

_____

Did you see buildings or houses? What were they like?

_____

_____

_____

What is unique about this vacation?

What were the top 5 activities you did in the national park?

1 _____

2 _____

3 _____

4 _____

5 _____

Paste, draw, doodle or write evidence of your exploration here:

JOURNAL WRITING

MY VACATION IN...

OVERALL RATING:

Tell us a story abour your vacation. WHEN did you go on your trip? WHERE did you visit? WHO were you with? WHAT did you do?

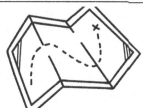

MY EXPLORATION REPORT:

During vacation, what was the weather like?

_____

_____

Listen closely. What 3 nature sounds can you hear?

1 _____

2 _____

3 _____

Look around. What 3 animals or insects do you see?

1 _____

2 _____

3 _____

Did you see a body of water? What was it like?

_____

_____

Did you see buildings or houses? What were they like?

_____

_____

_____

What is unique about this vacation?

What were the top 5 activities you did in the national park?

1 _____

2 _____

3 _____

4 _____

5 _____

Paste, draw, doodle or write evidence of your exploration here:

JOURNAL WRITING

MY VACATION IN...

OVERALL RATING:

Tell us a story abour your vacation. WHEN did you go on your trip? WHERE did you visit? WHO were you with? WHAT did you do?

MY EXPLORATION REPORT:

During vacation, what was the weather like?

_____

_____

Listen closely. What 3 nature sounds can you hear?

1 _____

2 _____

3 _____

Look around. What 3 animals or insects do you see?

1 _____

2 _____

3 _____

Did you see a body of water? What was it like?

_____

_____

Did you see buildings or houses? What were they like?

_____

_____

_____

What is unique about this vacation?

What were the top 5 activities you did in the national park?

1 _____

2 _____

3 _____

4 _____

5 _____

Paste, draw, doodle or write evidence of your exploration here:

JOURNAL WRITING

MY VACATION IN...

OVERALL RATING:

Tell us a story abour your vacation. WHEN did you go on your trip? WHERE did you visit? WHO were you with? WHAT did you do?

MY EXPLORATION REPORT:

During vacation, what was the weather like?

_____

_____

Listen closely. What 3 nature sounds can you hear?

1 _____

2 _____

3 _____

Look around. What 3 animals or insects do you see?

1 _____

2 _____

3 _____

Did you see a body of water? What was it like?

_____

_____

Did you see buildings or houses? What were they like?

_____

_____

_____

What is unique about this vacation?

Paste, draw, doodle or write evidence of your exploration here:

What were the top 5 activities you did in the national park?

1 _____

2 _____

3 _____

4 _____

5 _____

JOURNAL WRITING

MY VACATION IN...

OVERALL RATING:

Tell us a story abour your vacation. WHEN did you go on your trip? WHERE did you visit? WHO were you with? WHAT did you do?

MY EXPLORATION REPORT:

During vacation, what was the weather like?

_____

_____

Listen closely. What 3 nature sounds can you hear?

1 _____

2 _____

3 _____

Look around. What 3 animals or insects do you see?

1 _____

2 _____

3 _____

Did you see a body of water? What was it like?

_____

_____

Did you see buildings or houses? What were they like?

_____

_____

_____

What is unique about this vacation?

What were the top 5 activities you did in the national park?

1 _____

2 _____

3 _____

4 _____

5 _____

Paste, draw, doodle or write evidence of your exploration here:

SCRAPBOOKING

Use these pages to sketch, doodle, or paste keepsakes like photos, tickets, stamps, leaves or other things to remember your vacations by.

SCRAPBOOKING

Use these pages to sketch, doodle, or paste keepsakes like photos, tickets, stamps, leaves or other things to remember your vacations by.

SCRAPBOOKING

Use these pages to sketch, doodle, or paste keepsakes like photos, tickets, stamps, leaves or other things to remember your vacations by.

SCRAPBOOKING

Use these pages to sketch, doodle, or paste keepsakes like photos, tickets, stamps, leaves or other things to remember your vacations by.

SCRAPBOOKING

Use these pages to sketch, doodle, or paste keepsakes like photos, tickets, stamps, leaves or other things to remember your vacations by.

SCRAPBOOKING

Use these pages to sketch, doodle, or paste keepsakes like photos, tickets, stamps, leaves or other things to remember your vacations by.

SCRAPBOOKING

Use these pages to sketch, doodle, or paste keepsakes like photos, tickets, stamps, leaves or other things to remember your vacations by.

SCRAPBOOKING

Use these pages to sketch, doodle, or paste keepsakes like photos, tickets, stamps, leaves or other things to remember your vacations by.

SCRAPBOOKING

Use these pages to sketch, doodle, or paste keepsakes like photos, tickets, stamps, leaves or other things to remember your vacations by.

SCRAPBOOKING

Use these pages to sketch, doodle, or paste keepsakes like photos, tickets, stamps, leaves or other things to remember your vacations by.

SCRAPBOOKING

Use these pages to sketch, doodle, or paste keepsakes like photos, tickets, stamps, leaves or other things to remember your vacations by.

SCRAPBOOKING

Use these pages to sketch, doodle, or paste keepsakes like photos, tickets, stamps, leaves or other things to remember your vacations by.

SCRAPBOOKING

Use these pages to sketch, doodle, or paste keepsakes like photos, tickets, stamps, leaves or other things to remember your vacations by.

SCRAPBOOKING

Use these pages to sketch, doodle, or paste keepsakes like photos, tickets, stamps, leaves or other things to remember your vacations by.

SCRAPBOOKING

Use these pages to sketch, doodle, or paste keepsakes like photos, tickets, stamps, leaves or other things to remember your vacations by.

SCRAPBOOKING

Use these pages to sketch, doodle, or paste keepsakes like photos, tickets, stamps, leaves or other things to remember your vacations by.

SCRAPBOOKING

Use these pages to sketch, doodle, or paste keepsakes like photos, tickets, stamps, leaves or other things to remember your vacations by.

SCRAPBOOKING

Use these pages to sketch, doodle, or paste keepsakes like photos, tickets, stamps, leaves or other things to remember your vacations by.

SCRAPBOOKING

Use these pages to sketch, doodle, or paste keepsakes like photos, tickets, stamps, leaves or other things to remember your vacations by.

SCRAPBOOKING

*Use these pages to sketch, doodle, or paste keepsakes like photos, tickets, stamps,
leaves or other things to remember your vacations by.*

SCRAPBOOKING

Use these pages to sketch, doodle, or paste keepsakes like photos, tickets, stamps, leaves or other things to remember your vacations by.

SCRAPBOOKING

Use these pages to sketch, doodle, or paste keepsakes like photos, tickets, stamps, leaves or other things to remember your vacations by.

SCRAPBOOKING

Use these pages to sketch, doodle, or paste keepsakes like photos, tickets, stamps, leaves or other things to remember your vacations by.

SCRAPBOOKING

Use these pages to sketch, doodle, or paste keepsakes like photos, tickets, stamps, leaves or other things to remember your vacations by.

SCRAPBOOKING

Use these pages to sketch, doodle, or paste keepsakes like photos, tickets, stamps, leaves or other things to remember your vacations by.

Made in the USA
Monee, IL
12 June 2022

97883587R00070